The St. Lawrence Seaway

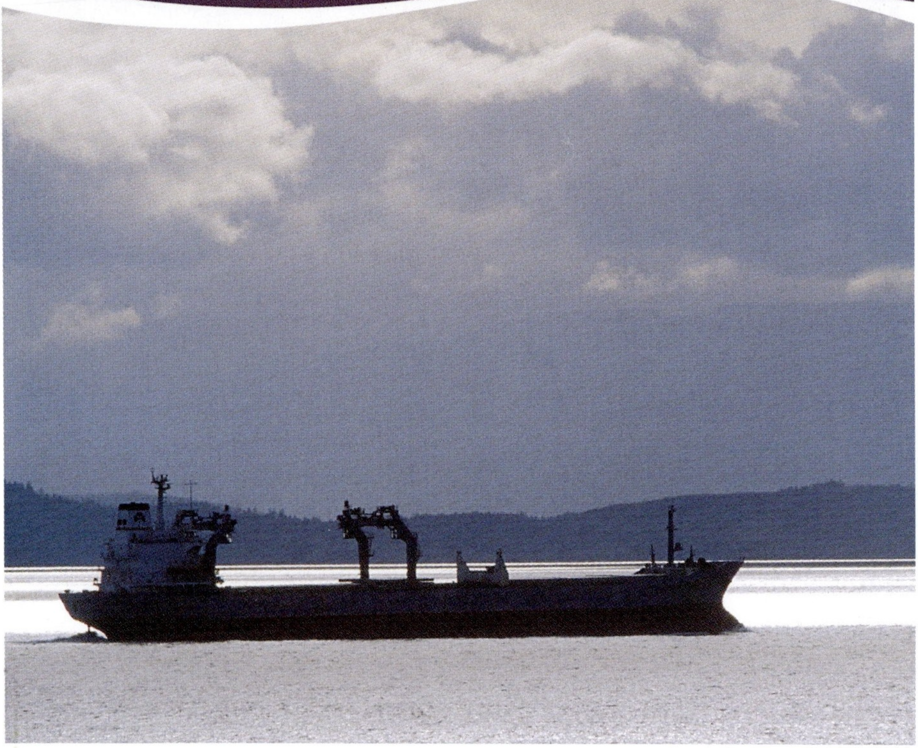

by Rebecca Perez

BOSTON

Map of the seaway from Montreal, Canada, to Lake Erie

The St. Lawrence Seaway is the world's largest inland waterway. It carries ocean vessels to cities deep inside Canada and the United States.

The seaway connects the Atlantic Ocean with the Great Lakes. It is largely formed by the St. Lawrence River flowing between the province of Quebec and the state of New York.

Vessel entering a lock on the St. Lawrence Seaway

Ships once had a hard time getting through the St. Lawrence River. They had to deal with fast-flowing rapids and changes in the height of the river. In the 1800s, Canada built canals and locks — "floating escalators" — to make it easier for ships to use the river.

Construction site of the St. Lawrence Seaway project

In 1951, Canada decided to make the St. Lawrence River deeper and easier for shipping. The United States joined Canada in 1954. Both countries wanted ocean-going ships to make it all the way to the Great Lakes. They also wanted the river to be able to handle more traffic.

They changed the average river depth from 14 feet to 27 feet. They also built locks, dams, and canals. The new 2,320-mile seaway opened in 1959. It cost $470 million. Canada paid about three fourths, the U.S. one fourth. Today, it takes only eight to ten days to travel from one end of the seaway to the other.

An aerial view of the St. Lawrence Seaway project

Lock gate opening in the Upper Beauharnois Lock, St. Lawrence Seaway, Quebec, Canada

There are nineteen locks on the St. Lawrence Seaway. They form the world's tallest water staircase. A lock is a canal with gates on either end. First ships go inside the lock. Then water is pumped in to raise the ships. It can also be pumped out to lower them. It takes about forty-five minutes for a ship to pass through a lock.

The ships on the seaway are called *lakers*. They are about 224 feet long on the average. They can hold up to 28,000 tons of goods. They can carry grain, corn, and other farm products. They also carry steel, iron, and heavy materials.

A Canadian laker and small boats on Lake Huron

A grain boat travelling through the Welland Canal

At the western end of the seaway is the Welland Canal. Ships need to cross the isthmus (a narrow strip of land) between Lake Ontario and Lake Erie. The only other way across is over Niagara Falls! Today eight locks lift ships over three hundred feet to reach Lake Erie. It makes a very dramatic ending to the St. Lawrence Seaway.